The Flower Children

...a story of Peace and Love and All Good Things!

Story by: Judith Kristen
Art by: William Kirkpatrick

Copyright © 2014, Judith Kristen & William Kirkpatrick. All rights reserved.
No part of this book may be reproduced, stored in a retrieval system,
or transmitted by any means without written permission from the publisher.
www.TheFlowerChildrenBook.com

ISBN-13: 978-0984950584
ISBN-10: 0984950583

This book is printed on acid-free paper.

Written by Judith Kristen
JudithKristen.com

Artwork by William Kirkpatrick
willebooks.carbonmade.com

This beautiful story was edited by Flower Children:

Susan Ryan (www.fab4nyctours.wordpress.com),

Miss Bobbie Bechtel,

and

Ms. Kristen Lauren Beisel.

This book is dedicated to
EVERY Flower Child - EVERYWHERE!

Once Upon a Time - not so long ago - in the 1960s, there were four teenage sisters.

They were the daughters of Mr. and Mrs. Aquinas Flower, and so they were known as...

The Flower Children.

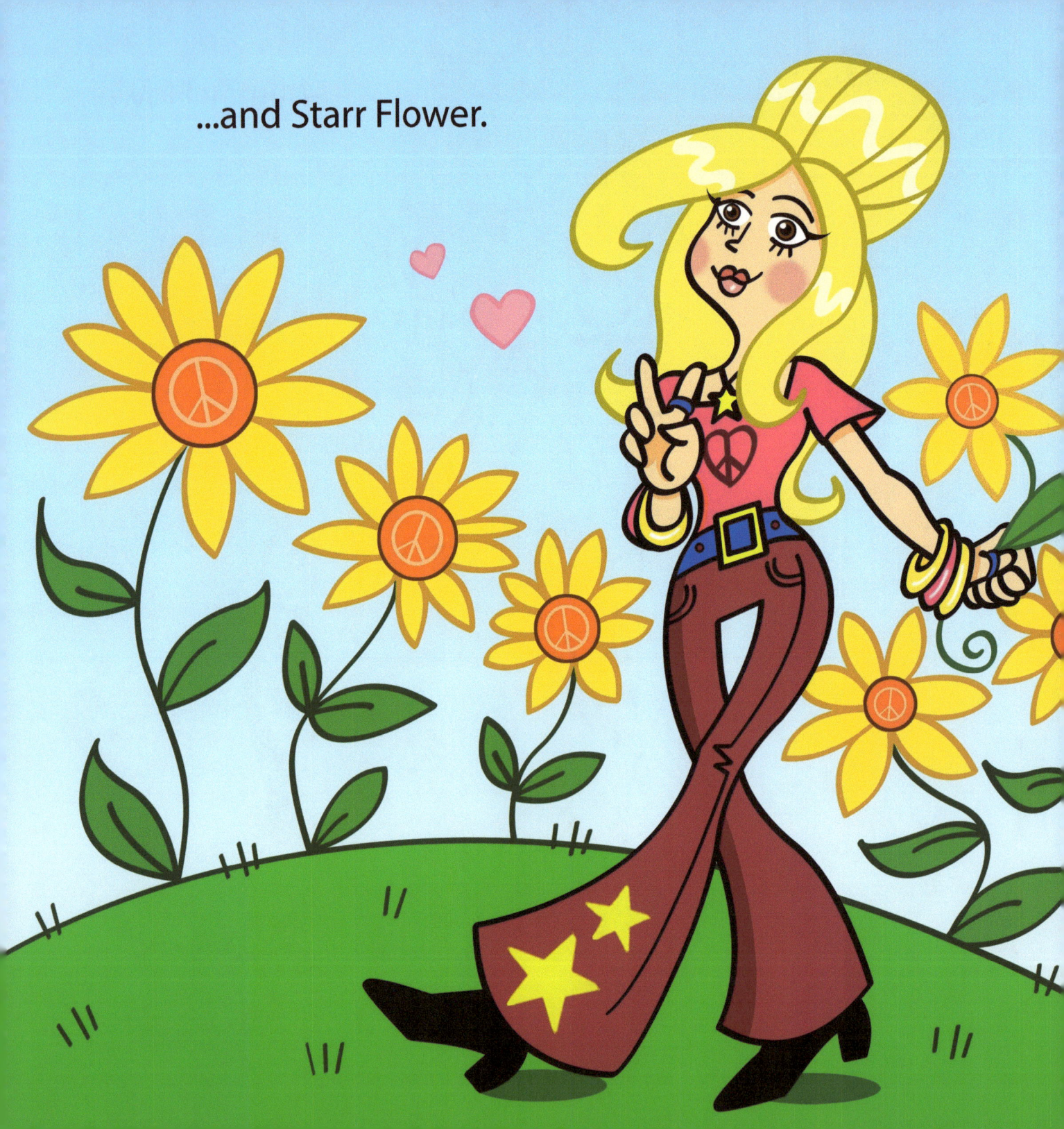

All four sisters were very kind and loving young girls.

They lived their lives with a strong sense of brotherhood, sisterhood, and neighborhood, and a vision to make the world a better place for everyone.

Isn't that nice?

By the way, they even had a little baby sister named Shelly Flower...

...and little Shelly was learning a LOT of wonderful things from her big sisters!

Each sister led by example. Jude was very creative. She loved to draw and design pretty little objects that she would give to her friends and family - just to make them smile.

Everyone loved Jude because she was so kind and thoughtful.

Donna loved the family garden and all its trees. Sometimes, Donna would sit down under a tall oak near the wishing well and sing some of her favorite songs.

Even the birds liked to listen to her sing!

Do you like to sing?

Mimsy Flower loved animals.
And the animals loved Mimsy.

Mimsy was always bringing a furry friend back home or looking for another nice family to care for a homeless dog or cat.

Even little Shelly helped whenever she could.

Wasn't that sweet?

Starr Flower loved to take photos of beautiful things, smiling faces, and fun-filled places. Sometimes, Starr would post her very best pictures all over town for everyone to see. That would bring a smile to those people's faces too!

That was a lot of fun for everyone!

The Flower Children knew that the good they were doing for others was something they wanted to do for the rest of their lives.

One day they gathered together to have a meeting in their backyard. Each sister vowed to always be kind and good-hearted and do whatever she could to spread peace and love and all good things wherever she went.

Time marched on and The Flower Children grew up - each girl keeping her teenage promise.

The sisters knew that a lot of teenagers in the 60s spoke of peace and love, but they also knew that it involved more than just "talk" to make all things bright and beautiful.

They knew that to make a change in the world one must BE the change they wished to see.

And The Flower Children saw to it that they did just that!

Jude Flower created lovely pieces of art in miniature. They were displayed in hundreds of galleries all over the world. Her beautiful "little" work was loved everywhere - and in a BIG, BIG way!

Donna Flower became a nurse and she took very good care of everyone. Sometimes she would sing to her patients - just to see them smile. And, the birds still liked to listen in.

Mimsy Flower became an author so that she could write books about being kind to animals.
Children and their parents loved Mimsy's stories.

I bet you could write a wonderful story about being kind to animals too!

Starr Flower became a professional photographer and toured the world looking for wonderful places and interesting people to photograph.

Everyone always smiled into the camera for Starr.

It's good to smile.

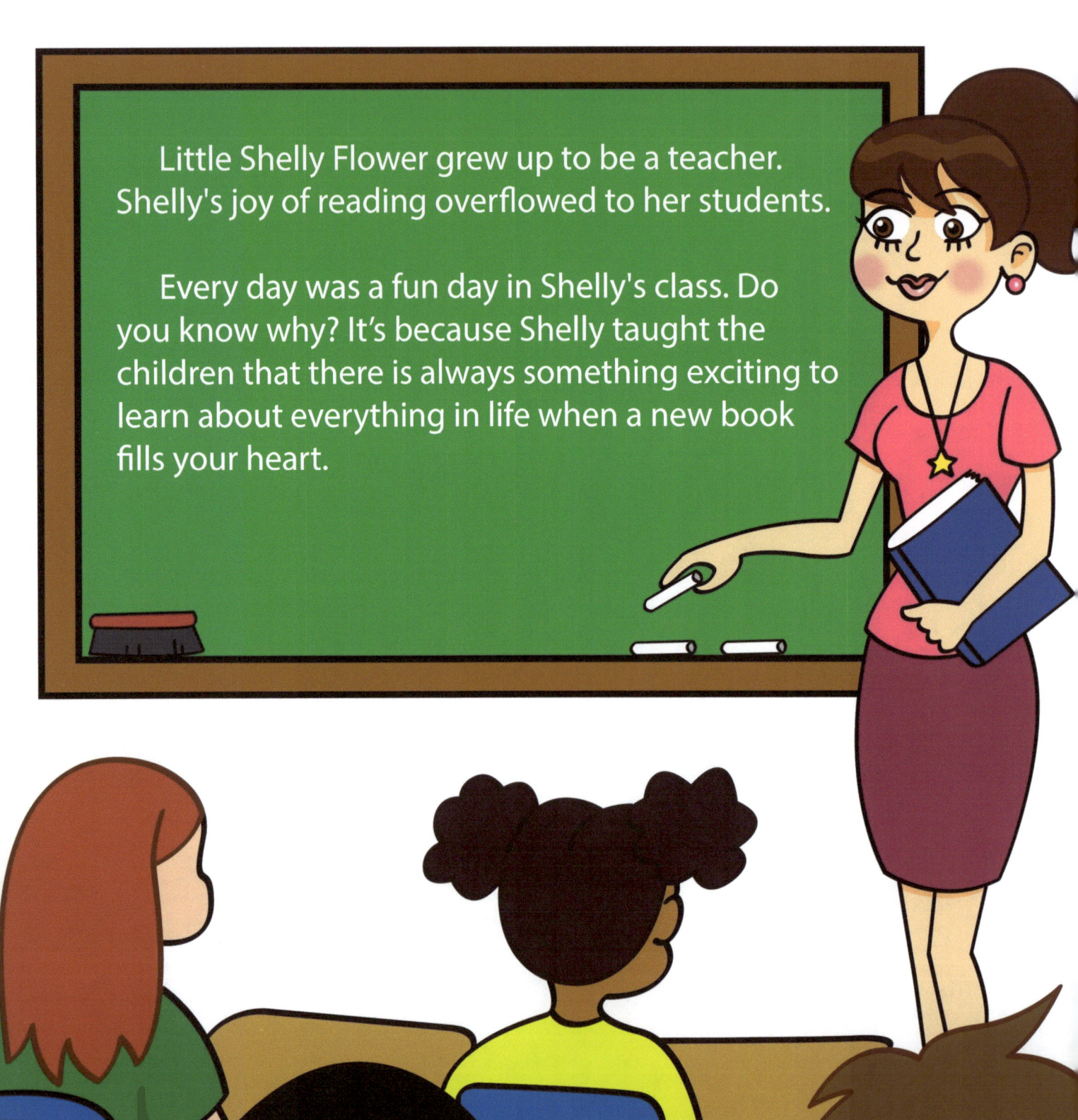

As the years passed, all of The Flower Children married wonderful, kind, and loving men. And soon they all had children of their own.

The "new" Flower Children learned by example. They were wonderful, kind, and loving too - just like their mothers and fathers.

To this very day, there are many Flower Children among us continuing to do good deeds. They are bringing smiles to people's faces, finding good homes for our animal friends, teaching children the joy of reading, and making the world a better, safer, healthier, and happier place for all of us.

If you could meet Jude, Donna, Starr, or Mimsy Flower, and they asked you about all of the good deeds you have done... what would you say?

I bet you could tell them LOTS of wonderful things that you've done to be kind and loving and helpful!

So, I guess that makes YOU a Flower Child too!!!!!

The End...?

www.ingramcontent.com/pod-product-compliance
Lightning Source LLC
Chambersburg PA
CBHW042124040426
42450CB00002B/63